40 Poems

By Rudy Thomas

Printed in the United States
Old Seventy Creek Press
2017

COPYRIGHT 2017 BY RUDY THOMAS

2017 OLD SEVENTY CREEK FIRST EDITION
PRINTED IN THE UNITED STATES OF AMERICA

ALL RIGHTS RESERVED UNDER INTERNATIONAL
AND PAN-AMERICAN COPYRIGHT CONVENTIONS

PUBLISHED IN THE UNITED STATES
BY OLD SEVENTY CREEK PRESS
RUDY THOMAS, PUBLISHER
P. O. BOX 204
ALBANY, KENTUCKY 42602

ISBN-13:978-0692723401
(Old Seventy Creek Press)
     ISBN-10:0692723404

*"All the perversions of the soul
I learnt on a small farm."*
    Michael Hartnett, Irish poet, 1941-1999

The last dream I had	page 1
A Poetry Publisher told me	page 2
Driving from Rice Subdivision	page 3
Written After Reading Anne Sexton's *The Awful Rowing Toward God* (1975)	page 4
Hot, humid Saturday	page 5
Praying Mantis	page 6
Text from Ange	page 7
I get up	page 8
Chester Johnson Poem One	page 10
Chester Johnson, Poem Two	page 11
Chester Johnson Three	page 12
Chester Johnson, Poem Four	page 13
Chester Johnson, Poem Five	page 14
Chester Johnson, Poem Six	page 15
Chester Johnson, Poem Seven	page 16
Chester Johnson, Poem Eight	page 17
Chester Johnson, Poem Nine	page 19
Chester Johnson, Poem Ten	page 20
Chester Johnson, Poem Eleven to be read down, & then across	page 21
Chester Johnson, Poem Twelve	page 22
Two young ladies on the sidewalk	page 23
The late-season cornfield	page 24
To Write	page 25

When sleep won't come	page 26
For Kathy before you stopped love	page 27
My Mother's Last Will and Testament	page 28
A Summer Poem	page 29
My Words	page 30
For Robert Polston	page 31
Two people on a cruise ship deck	page 33
Day One approaching the island Poros	page 34
Day Two on Poros	page 35
Day Three on Poros	page 36
Day Four on Poros	page 38
Day Five on Poros	page 40
Old Seventy Creek	page 42
Unsigned Thank You Note	page 44
She undressed for skinny dipping	page 45
I return	page 46
What did it really mean?	page 47

Special thanks go to Maureen Clifford,
Poetry Editor, *The Australia Times Poetry Magazine*, for publishing: *For Kathy before you stopped love* and *Praying Mantis* **in Vol. 5 No. 3, February 10, 2017.**

40 Poems

By Rudy Thomas

The last dream I had

My red haired father was in it.
My red haired brother was in it.
My oldest, red haired sister was in it.
My athletic, red haired sister was in it.
My black haired mother was in it.

What a joyful reunion we had in it
that dark night at Hilltop Cemetery.

No sweet scent of dessert wine
drifted through the night air.
No bourbon scent clung to the grass.

A whippoorwill sang in the valley
where blackberry briars took to bloom.
We would never again plant corn
on our Kentucky, rolling hillside farm.

A Poetry Publisher told me

"I never publish a poet who writes
in the first person. I don't care about I
enough to read the poem, &
I never publish a manuscript
by any poet who presumes
to put self above the rest of us," so
spoke the learned publisher.

Anne Sexton, he would not have published her,
ending **The Black Art,** how did it go:
Dear love, I am that girl. Perhaps he assumes
Walt Whitman's *I celebrate myself* too nondescript
to bloom on the page like lilacs for the last time &
who do I think that I am to write of you, what I
choose—butterfly that circles once—alights

upon my shoulder?

Driving from Rice Subdivision

Wind from the southwest
strips white blooms from Bradford Pears
that line the street.

Like large snowflakes in February,
they create a blizzard & fall,
covering grass in white.

I remember two winters in a row
when I lay on frozen ground,
ratting the sewer line.

I hear my father's voice
talking about men freezing to death
in the Battle of the Belgium Bulge.

At the stop sign while I wait,
I close my eyes.
The warmth of your skin,

while I massage your shoulders
& your neck, excites me...
The driver behind me honks--I open my eyes.

Written after Reading Anne Sexton's
The Awful Rowing Toward God (1975)

When woman
takes a man inside her
like a mole entering a tunnel,
going forward, backward,
& the man takes pleasure
& catches his breath
as he should,
one of them may cry out
& the woman with the man inside her,
allows no knot to be tied
so they cannot separate
like dogs conjoined
& the woman climbs the mountain
of her orgasm
& the man goes
as deep into her darkness as he can.

The woman,
the man
with their twin desires
do not fear God,
for briefly they feel immortal,
but God in His Heaven
knows who let them learn
that they were naked
in His Garden.

Hot, humid Saturday

For two hours yesterday,
I cleaned the gutter
in front of your house.

You were not at home.
I cannot begin to say
how unpleasant the day was.

How unbearably hot it was,
& miserable in every way,
me scooping decaying organic loam

like human waste from an outhouse.
How I would have traded my job for a fish gutter's
chore in those minutes, but when a

wren flew from your hanging flowerpot
& scolded me, I smiled a smile
meant only for me.

When a red wasp darted at me,
I did not think. I let my rile
control my action. My swat

missed;
its did not.

Praying Mantis

Winter was fast approaching
when I found you in the forest.
Black clouds, intermingled with cold
air white clouds, foretold you demise.

The encroaching
storm, I thought, would be the test
of your survival. Would you take hold
of my outstretched finger & be wise?

That was the question I asked myself.
To my surprise, you crawled onto my hand;
I took you to my house & fed you hamburger
until spring returned to Old Seventy Creek.

At home, I took your jar from the shelf
above my nightstand.
I emptied the final bits of hamburger
& hoped the females you would seek

by following their sex pheromones
would not devour you before nightfall.

Text from Ange

Happiness is short lived
in the human world;
in our very own world.

Live for the moment
and embrace life
whether it is at its finest

or at its worst.
Life is short
in its journey.

We have no promise
the sun will always
rise in the morning.

Fear not the dark.
If it fades, know the sun shines,
elsewhere giving life a full, new meaning.

I get up

It is not dawn
by four hours.
A poem has begun
its labor pains.

False labor pains,
a poem in a web spun
with thin words, their powers
addictive as a yawn;

captive nonetheless
am I, insomnia keeping
me in the middle
of it the way love

has done before, only love
with the high-pitches of a fiddle
can do once more, creeping

out of my mind
into my write.

Sailors abandoning the USS Lexington after the ship was hit by torpedoes on May 8, 1942.

Chester Johnson, Poem One

I am not a mayfly.
If you know anything about that insect,
you will understand what separates us
other than me being human
and the mayfly being
an insect with one sole purpose:
Eat food, breed and then die.

All God's creatures have a purpose.
What more can a human say?

Chester Johnson, Poem Two

I was born down the street from where I live now
in a white house just past a flower shop.
There is no house there now.

I lived there until I was 13—really 12 and a half,
and then I went to the CCC camp
at Stearns, Kentucky.

I have a cap up there above my bookcase—the one
in the middle. It represents
my time at the CCC camp.

The other two caps there
represent my service on two ships
of all the ones I sailed on.

After my time
with the CCC camp expired,
they told us we were going to the National Guard.

Chester Johnson Three

I told the CO that day at Stearns,
"I don't want to be in the National Guard."
I said, "my father served in the Navy and
I wanted to join the Navy, too."

I did not want to go
for training at Fort Knox, Kentucky.
CO gave me a letter and told me
to take it to a Navy recruiter.

They sent me from Stearns to Somerset, Kentucky.
From there, I made my way home.
A Navy recruiter came to Albany
and signed me up.

Chester Johnson, Poem Four

I don't know
if I want you
to write much about my service.

I still have terrible dreams
about the things I saw.
It's unspeakable what we had to do.

It's ungodly what they had to do.
We were young.
I will be 92 years old soon.

I have diabetic feet.
I walk as much as I can
just to keep myself going.

When I told my doctor about my memories,
he told me to go to the VA,
for they know how to deal with such things.

Patton never believed a military man
could be shell shocked during World War II.
Now they just call it some initials.

I never went to the VA.
You see they would have wanted
to do mental tests on me just to call me crazy.

Chester Johnson, Poem Five

I went to the Navy in 1942.
I served in World War II,
the Korean War they say was not a war,
and I served in the Vietnam War.

I was at Guadalcanal
and on the *USS Missouri*
as a Petty Officer Third Class
from the *USS Iowa* on September 2, 1945.

I was there to help wire
a sound system that would be used
by General McArthur. Tojo was there.
I was up on the crowded, second deck

of the battleship,
looking down
on the signing event.
It's still hard for me

to grasp
how Truman's two bombs
changed
our world forever.

Chester Johnson, Poem Six

I don't want to make it appear
that I was in charge of anything,
or that I was more important
than the other sailors
who helped wire the sound system.
With so many dignitaries coming
for the signing, a number of sailors
from the *USS Missouri* were temporarily stationed
on the *USS Iowa* for the duration of the surrender
ceremony which took place aboard the *Missouri*.
I know there is no way to find out who helped me,
but as I told you I was not assigned
to the *USS Missouri*.
I was assigned to the *USS Iowa*,
a Petty Officer Third Class
and I was ordered to go
from the *Iowa* to the *Missouri*.

Chester Johnson, Poem Seven

I can't begin to tell you
how much strength our military showed
for the signing occasion.
Maybe that picture up there on the wall
will give you a way
to judge the importance of the event
that was unfolding before my eyes.

Chester Johnson, Poem Eight

Say the kids are good.
And Joyce?
I'd like to see her.

Say you were here
three times
and couldn't wake me.

Other people say
they've come and knocked
on my storm door.

I sleep sound in this chair.
I can't hear good.
I have to turn the tv up loud.

I'll tell you what you do.
Next time that happens
there's a string out there.

See that bell up there.
It's from the USS Lexington.
You pull that string and I'll hear it.

It brings back the past when it chimes.
My memory is full of youth,
full of shock waves in the sea

when we fired the big guns.
I say *we* not *I* or *me*.
In battle we were one.

Of course
you can take a picture
of it.

Chester Johnson, Poem Nine

So you asked what a flagship is.
The *USS Iowa* was a fast ship,
a fast battleship.

It was heavily armed
and the lead ship for the Pacific
Theater of War.

When Vice Admiral Willis A. Lee,
or another Admiral was on board,
we raised a special flag.

When the Admiral's flag flew,
the *USS Iowa* was a flagship.
It wasn't complicated.

The *Iowa* flew
Admiral Bull Halsey's flag,
for the Japanese surrender ceremony.

Chester Johnson, Poem Ten

I remember the first time
I saw a *kamikaze*
hit one of ours.

I thought:
*how senseless a thing
for a pilot to do.*

I didn't have long
to think though...
three came for the *Iowa*.

I can't take credit for it,
but I could be thankful
our gunners knocked out

two Jills and a Judy
on the way
to sink us.

Since you ask,
a Jill was a Jap
carrier dive bomber.

A Judy was a Jap
torpedo bomber
we'd meet them again

in the skies over Okinawa.

**Chester Johnson, Poem Eleven
to be read down, & then across**

Thanks for the fruit basket.	the Twin Towers
I appreciate the offer	brought down
of dinner.	by a new enemy.
It's Father's Day.	Two planes,
I'm waiting for my daughter	direct hits
to come from Tennessee.	exploding,
I'll eat a banana	I watched
before she comes,	smoke--
and to answer that question:	saw
Was I ever afraid?	people
I was trained	abandon
not to have emotions.	ship,
Yes, just like a doctor	f
as an intern learns	a
to deal with death.	l
Kamikazes	l
were like staring	i
death in the face.	n
I didn't think	g
I'd feel that tight,	ahead
gut-wrenching	of that
determination	terrible swift
to live again	sword. I'll eat
until I watched	that banana now.

Chester Johnson, Poem Twelve

You have to remember that it's been
74 years now since I went to sea.
My pay grade was E4,
Petty Officer Third Class at the signing.

When I got my patch,
it was tacked on my sleeve;
the eagle was called a crow.
I was punched half a dozen times,

hearty punches that bruised my arm.
I was lucky no one tacked me
with that needle.
I was as happy as I could be, however,

for I had achieved the lowest grade
of noncommissioned officer.
Neither my achievements,
nor my crow ever flew away.

Two young ladies on the sidewalk

I stop & wait while they walk
down the hill toward me.
It is not the first time
young ladies have reminded me
of Michael Hartnett who grew up
in the Maiden Street area of Newcastle
West in old County Limerick,
Ireland.
The irony of Michael's Limerick
birthplace is that he became a poet.
The irony of his poetry
to younger women
is the way he vents his anger
for his own mistakes,
addresses his daughter,
but advances his mastery
of the line.

The two young ladies
on the sidewalk
and his poetry
mostly written out of love
when he was a sad,
lonely man
have little to do with me
unless the title of one
of his books
counts for something.
In contrast to Michael,
I am happy
when I see them behind me.
I am thankful that
all the perversions of my soul
I never learned on a small dairy farm.

The late-season cornfield

I see it to my left, a cornfield, recently planted
near Highway 61, sweet corn sprouts an inch tall
in red clay, Kentucky soil.
I keep driving south toward Burkesville.

The nightjar sang, *whip-poor-will*,
in early May, warning farmers to till & toil;
singing *time to plant corn*; its nocturnal call
although unheeded due to rains; it never recanted.

I make a quick turnaround;
pull off the road;
enter the cornfield;
walk row after row.

The field is not fertile ground
like Cumberland River bottom land. A road
once ran the length of it, revealed
by limestone gravel on clay. I turn to go

back toward my car, and say:
"there you are," as soon as I see
the corner-notched arrowhead,
speckled Kentucky flint washed clean,

by yesterday's rain.

To Write

I never had to leave the place
I called home, nor forget the community
where my beliefs, values, concepts
originated. I am the product of my environment.

I never gave up my speech,
nor changed my face,
nor regretted my uneven landscape intercepts
in favor of a greater society's torment.

I never fought positive change to the land
I love. I fought the idea of making an escape
to some other place; I have gone in search of self,
ridge to ridge, on foreign soil, but more

& more words take me inward,
images, feelings unite on the landscape
of my soul that defines me, has me assert myself
that I, without wings, may soar

& be
& become
& give form
to the voice I always heard.

When sleep won't come

I am not finished with the poem
that begs to be written
so I rise to darkness,
putting aside the chance
to dream of you.

It is not the ending of the poem
with which I am smitten;
it is the beginning's untidiness,
the hook I cannot dangle; it is not romance
that is lacking; it is you.

For Kathy before you stopped loving

It is this picture I have of you
that endures.
You bend over the sink.
You do not see my smile.

I do not speak
though I wonder why
you are up so early
& our daughter sleeps near me.

I lust after your body.
I feel no shame.
When you wipe shampoo
from your eyelids, you take me.

You wrap a towel around your head.
you see me as though for the first time.
Words race across the page of my heart.
You come to me.

You place our daughter to the right,
making room for yourself.
You put your head on my shoulder.
You whisper into my ear:

"I hate you now;
I will hate you forever."
You get up; return to the bathroom,
& close the door.

My Mother's Last Will and Testament

Item One:
I direct that all my just debts,
upon which I have a legal description,
including my funeral expenses, the expenses
of my last illness, and the expense of the
administration of my estate be paid by my
Executor, hereinafter named,
out of the first monies coming into its hands
and available therefore.

Item Two:
I hereby give, devise and bequeath
unto Gary Thomas a .22 Rifle.

Item Three:
There are nine items in my home which are
numbered and David M. Cross, attorney
for the Estate is hereby directed to place
numbers 1-9 to be put in a hat
and let each of my children draw out a number
and that is the number they shall receive.

Item Four:
I hereby give, devise, and bequeath all the rest
of my estate of every kind and description,
wheresoever situated, of which I may die possessed
or over which I have the power of disposition or any
interest in whatsoever to be sold privately by a
method to be selected by my Co-Executor, and the
proceeds to be divided equally and alike as follows:
1/9 share of same to each of my 9 children.

A Summer Poem

I walk past the thorn tree.
wet with rainwater, a sagging limb
with a thorn sticks into my head.

Before I have bled,
I shake the branch I should trim.
A startled dove leaves her nest. She

brings a moment of rejoicing,
me for poetry, love, & hope--
she for new life, calling out from her nest.

My Words

My words cling to places
I know intimately
as though they would women
were they wet t shirts.

My words call out to me
like quail from the grown up
farm across the road
from the farm I grew up on.

My words look back at me
from the page like authentic arrowheads
from Kentucky red clay fields
or black dirt river bottoms.

Robert Polston

You took a legacy with you
to Peolia, to that place
where your voice is muffled
beneath black granite.

Someone knocked down
your tombstone,
the separate parts felled
like tree limbs in a storm.

It will soon be November,
the month your supporters
would go out from your garage
in the dark of night to do your bidding.

One night I sat with you in your dark showroom
while you watch traffic flow past
like Old Seventy Creek on its course
to 76 Falls.

You asked about my father.
You called him the best friend
you ever had.
I thanked you for that.

I asked you about Munich.
You stood up; tugged your trousers;
cursed your nephew;
and Ned, the Chairman of the Board

of Education for losing control.
"If a man won't help his family," you said,
he won't help anyone.
Hell! I bombed Munich.

I looked down on that city
through bombsights at explosions
orange in pitch dark like flashing turn signals.
You have to watch Dallas.

Jerome and Ned
should have voted for you
to get that job."
I didn't apply," I said.

"What have you ever done to Ned?"
I can't tell him the real truth,
but I tell him one,
"Someone told him I'm too close to Hoyt."

"And he said you are too close to me."
You shook my hand.
"I've never denied you," I said.
"Don't ever mention this," you said.

You died.
Ned died.
Jerome recently died.
I keep trying to get Dallas to write.

Two people on a cruise ship deck

I thought I could write
words from my heart
when I was too young
to go to war
or buy beer.

I wish I could write
words from my heart
as lean as the young woman
who sat with me on the deck
of a cruise ship in a hurricane.

While I wondered if we would
ever reach Santorini, she shivered
in my arms, and told me:
you are the bravest man
I've ever met.

Day One approaching the island of Poros

As we approach the Greek island,
our tour guide tells us
it never rains on Poros.

A black cloud hangs over us.
The azure sea beneath the hydrofoil
is calm, blue to the end of its depth.

Before the hydrofoil leaves
with passengers from the island,
returning to Athens, the storm hits.

Lightning strikes in rapid protest,
chases me from the hotel balcony.
Through glass, I watch torrents

fall & run downhill
to pond in the front entrance
below.

Day Two on Poros

I explore the island
from the dock
to the top of the hill
beside or hotel.

I carve my initials
on a tree, the tallest one
past Zorba's Taverna
& mine are the only ones.

The cliff, behind the tree,
drops from its edge
to the seashore where rocks
catch incoming waves.

It is a process that has gone
undeterred, unlike romance,
for as long as cliff
& shoreline have existed.

I hear a woman wailing.
I see her at a grave
in the cemetery near me.
I move on in silence.

Day Three on Poros

I write poetry.
I eat lunch at a dockside
café, moussaka, white wine,
coarse bread, & feta cheese.

Other tourists move antlike
through the shops nearest the sea
until shop owners close
for their 2-5 o'clock fiesta.

The heat reminds me of Kentucky
except without the oppressive humidity.
At night, the men will come out
to dance & drink in a taverna.

I follow their lead,
& sleep for the afternoon in a room cooled
even temperature by thick walls,
whitewashed to deflect the sunlight.

When the sea absorbs its share
of heat, I will come out
& move up the hill
toward whatever merriment waits.

At midnight, I go down to the dock,
give my Campari & orange to a young
woman, perched on a wall, crying into
the dark night and the cool air from the sea.

She gives me a sea smooth rock
in return. "Did you hear my song flung
up to you? I've never had this drink you
scoundrel," she said. "It won't get me

drunk enough to go to bed with you."
I say nothing and she asks, "Will you
grant me one wish tonight, gentle fool?"
I hear a stronger voice, in her request.

"Unless a poem will satisfy you,
I cannot promise more. As poet, I do
words better than grant fantasies, beautiful
siren, & if that is the object of your quest,

I will begin."
"No," she says. I will wish for poetry
tomorrow. Tonight I have finished my song.
I want to dance like a southern gypsy.

"Only then
will I grant your one wish; the poetry
you write must be what has gone wrong
in my life, so far nothing good, you'll see."

Day Four on Poros

I walk toward the sea,
early while the city sleeps.
My internal clock would buzz saw
me awake at daybreak as it was set to do
in my youth. Every day of the week,
it would wake me, for I was the one
to bring the cows to the milk shed.
I was the one to milk the cows
before the school bus ran
in the morning, and after school,
for my father drove the bus.

I never raised a fuss,
not about milking or school,
not about plowing the mule, Dan--
not about being too bone weary to carouse,
to be with girls except in my head,
where my dreams would hit a homerun
every time. One day in Old Seventy Creek,
my sister's friend lost her halter top, two
pink nipples dropped my jaw
& she did not deny my curious peeps
nor knew that I memorized lines of poetry.

From the wall I watch small fry dine
on sewage, piped straight from the hotel
into the Mediterranean Sea with no regard
by management for polluting water as vast
as that sea.

A small sailboat docks near me.
A fisherman waves for me as fast
as he can, and points his scarred
hand into the boat. I get in. We sail.
He speaks no English; I no Greek. His wine

is warn, sweet & white.
The sky is blue to its height.

Day Five on Poros

I walk down to the docks again
in the morning, hoping to go to sea
again with the old fisherman.

It is not to be, for the fisherman
has a young man with him who approaches me,
"Thanks for helping him," he said, his English plain

& proper. "You should return
to your home; sell everything you own,
& come back to Poros & our sea.

Grandfather says you are surely
good luck. He always sails alone;
you gave his life a good turn.

The squid will wait.
Grandfather will yearn
to have his good luck charm back.

If you choose to come back
with the money you earn
from all your things, Fate

will smile on you
like a woman in love.
Here, you can live like royalty."

On the hydrofoil in the afternoon, royalty
Poros, the old man, blue sky above—
Athens ahead—reality breaks through:

before another morning dawns on Poros,
I will be at my job in Kentucky
& the young lady who granted my wish

& the old squid fisherman
will be separate,
not unequal memories.

Old Seventy Creek

Old
Seventy
Creek,
a
flow
in
my
memory—
its
cold
water
out
of
banks
in
spring—
almost
dry
in
times
of
drought—
the
place
I
learned
to
swim—
the
place
of
baptisms—
its
pools

deep
where
snail
darters
having
no
knowledge
of
what
extinction
means
for
a
species
hide
beneath
its
stones.

Unsigned Thank You Note

I always love reading your poetry.
You express things in words
that tug at my heartstrings.
You make everything shine
in its own brilliance.
I just wanted to tell you
what a wonderful poet you are.

I love your choices in both words
and style.
You never cease to make any poem
beautiful to read.
Emotions is what makes art.

You are an inspiration to me
 even at 3:30 in the morning.
I'm drunk on wine and words.
I apologize,
but I needed to say these things.

She undressed for skinny dipping

I wait in the cold, deep pool
beneath a waterfalls.
She turns toward me
& touches one toe
quickly
into the water,
creating concentric circles.

She pulls her toe out,
dripping one,
two,
three drops
into the blue pool.

She dresses
& walks uphill
toward her car.

I sit in the water
while shade overtakes
sunlight.

It was as close
to exchanging
the dizziness
of inside
& outside spaces
as we ever came.

In the passing of time,
I have become a poet.
My words, like water,
seek their own level.

I return

No longer young
& wild,
I return to that waterfall alone.
The scene is the same.
The water is cold to my finger
when I push it beneath the surface.
Concentric circle move out.

I do not undress.
I return,
for in a dream
she came flirting,
touching me until a fire burned,
until a desire to write poetry
woke me to an empty room.

I return.
She never pressed her naked body
against mine, even in the dream.
I look up the hill
& the same slant of light
that led me to stitch words together
the first time she left,
falls over me.

What did it really mean?

You walked away.
Was it lust you could not give in to?
Was it a test you put yourself through?
Were you ashamed of feeling seductive?

Reading poetry
is how I came to appreciate it.
Poetry is what it is
& many attempt to write it.

I write this poem
far from the cold, blue pool.
You are a warm memory
& that bottle of wine I drank

without you
still burns my soul.

www.ingramcontent.com/pod-product-compliance
Lightning Source LLC
Chambersburg PA
CBHW031431040426
42444CB00006B/764